Mama Never Told Me...™

Mama Never Told Me...™

A diary of unbelievable comments and questions posed to a pregnant woman

by Emily Van Do

illustrations by g.f. Newland

Copyright © 2009 Emily Van Do

Published by: Mama Never Told Me, LLC

All rights reserved. No part of this publication may be reproduced, stored in a retrieval system or transmitted, in any form, or by any means, electronic, mechanical, recorded, photocopied, or otherwise, without the prior permission of the copyright owner, except by a reviewer who may quote brief passages in a review.

Illustrations by: g.f. Newland
First Printing August 2009

Printed in the United States of America

ISBN:978-0-615-20294-5

To Maddox & Kiet ...

   without you, none of these intrusive questions
   and inappropriate comments would be possible ...

      and I wouldn't change any of it!

At 36 years old, I became pregnant for the first time. It was all of the things you would imagine - exciting and scary. It was also all of the things you wouldn't imagine.

I gained close to 60 pounds. On a 5'2" frame, that's a lot of extra weight. My husband didn't mind. I didn't mind. We were both so thrilled we were having a baby.

When you get pregnant, there are all of these books to help you out... how to deal with the pregnancy, what to expect - even a book about what the father should expect. What you won't find in a bookstore, however, is what happens to other people while you are pregnant.

Suddenly, people (mostly co-workers, strangers) decide they have free reign in commenting on your appearance. They have no issues touching your belly or pointing out the unavoidable and beautiful transformation your body endures while pregnant. If you appear annoyed or agitated then you are being hormonal. You are forced to try to laugh and bear it.

The comments were so outrageous that I started writing them down.

If you're reading this and you're pregnant, it will make you aware of what you're about to face.

                  I quickly realized that labor was nothing.

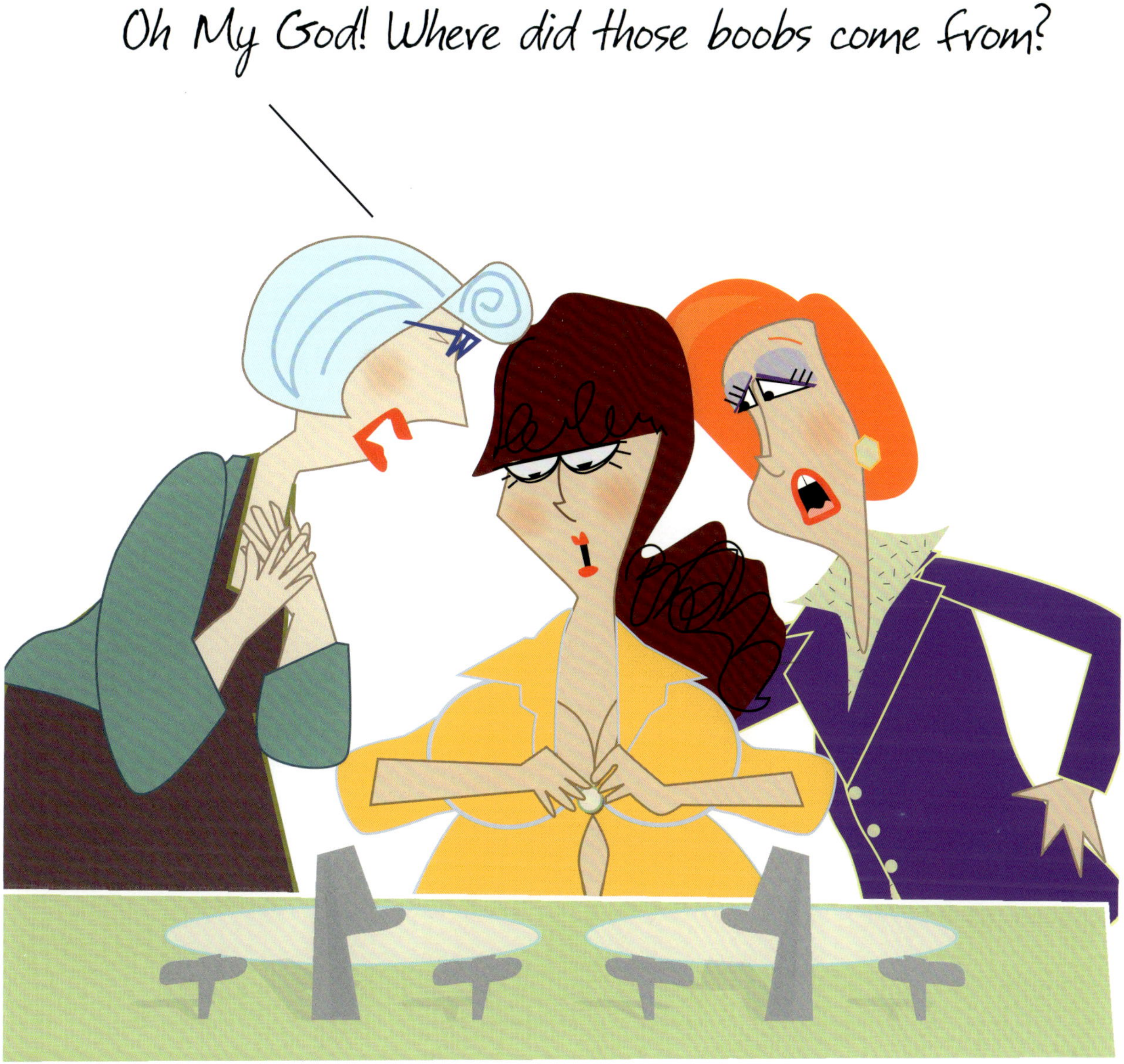
Oh My God! Where did those boobs come from?

"You know, you didn't have a big ass before, but now you do!"

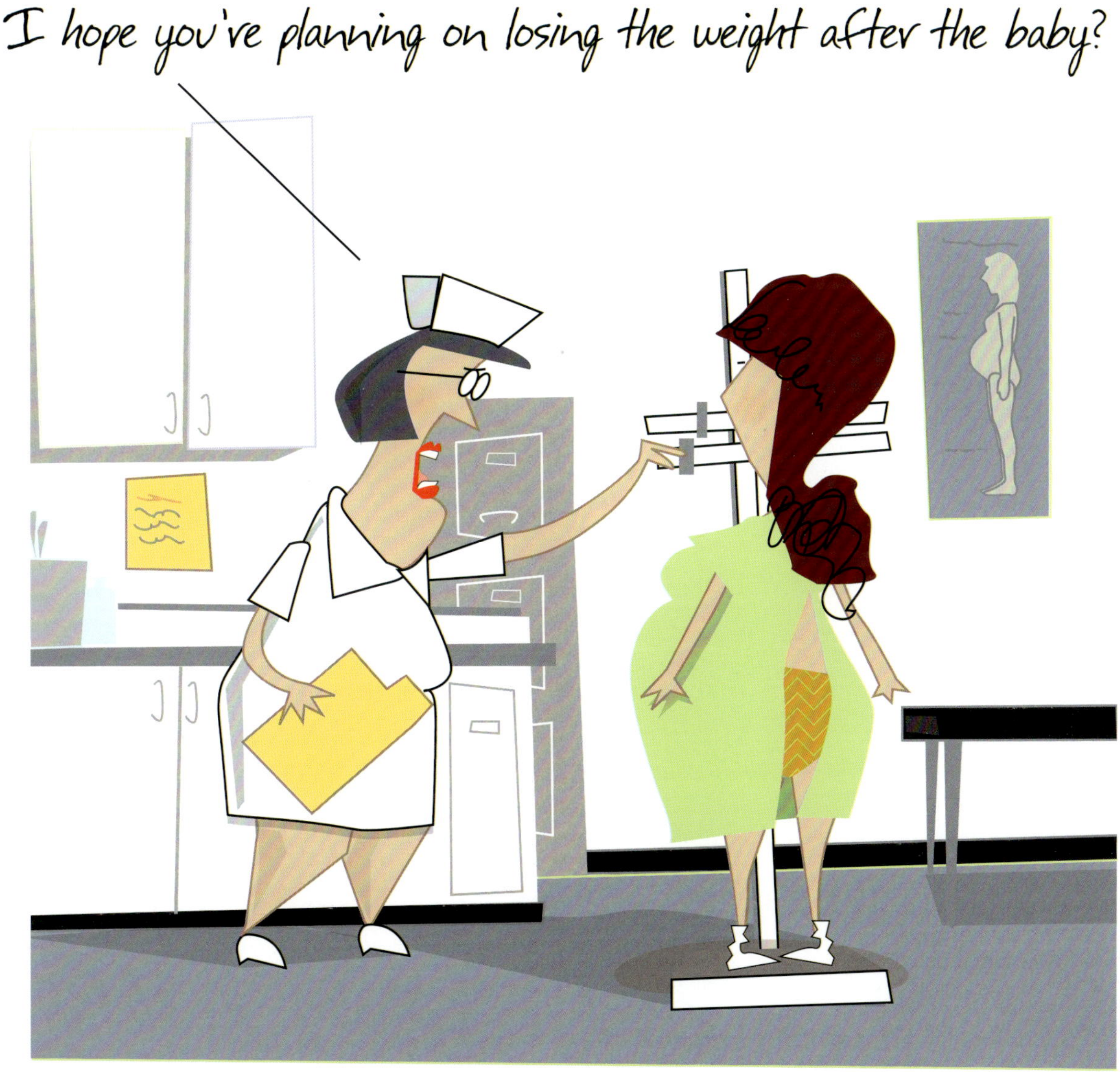
I hope you've planning on losing the weight after the baby?

You and Karen are due at the same time, but you are so much bigger!

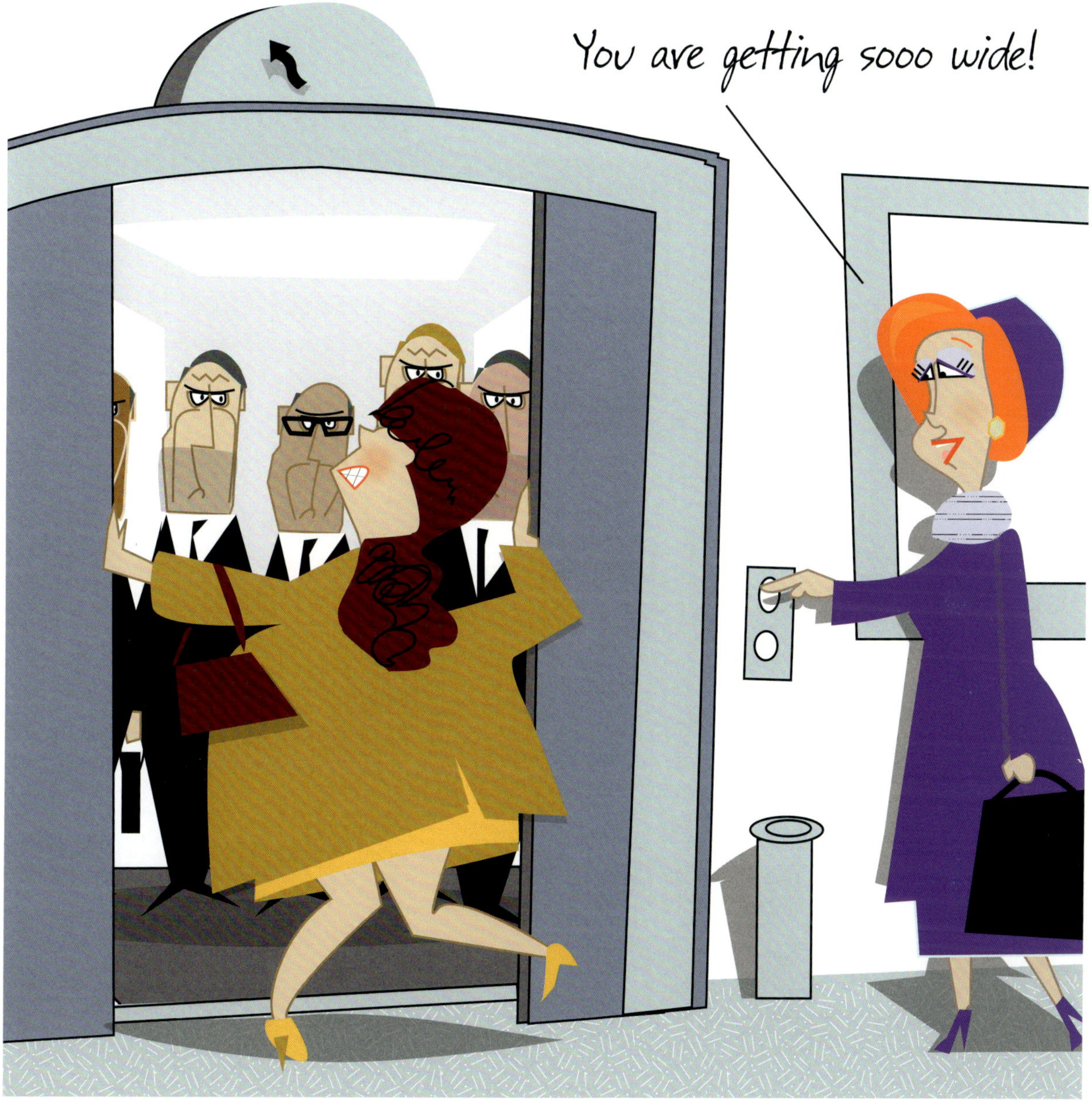
You are getting sooo wide!

I'm concerned that you are eating too much!
DELI
Sale $$$
Free Samples

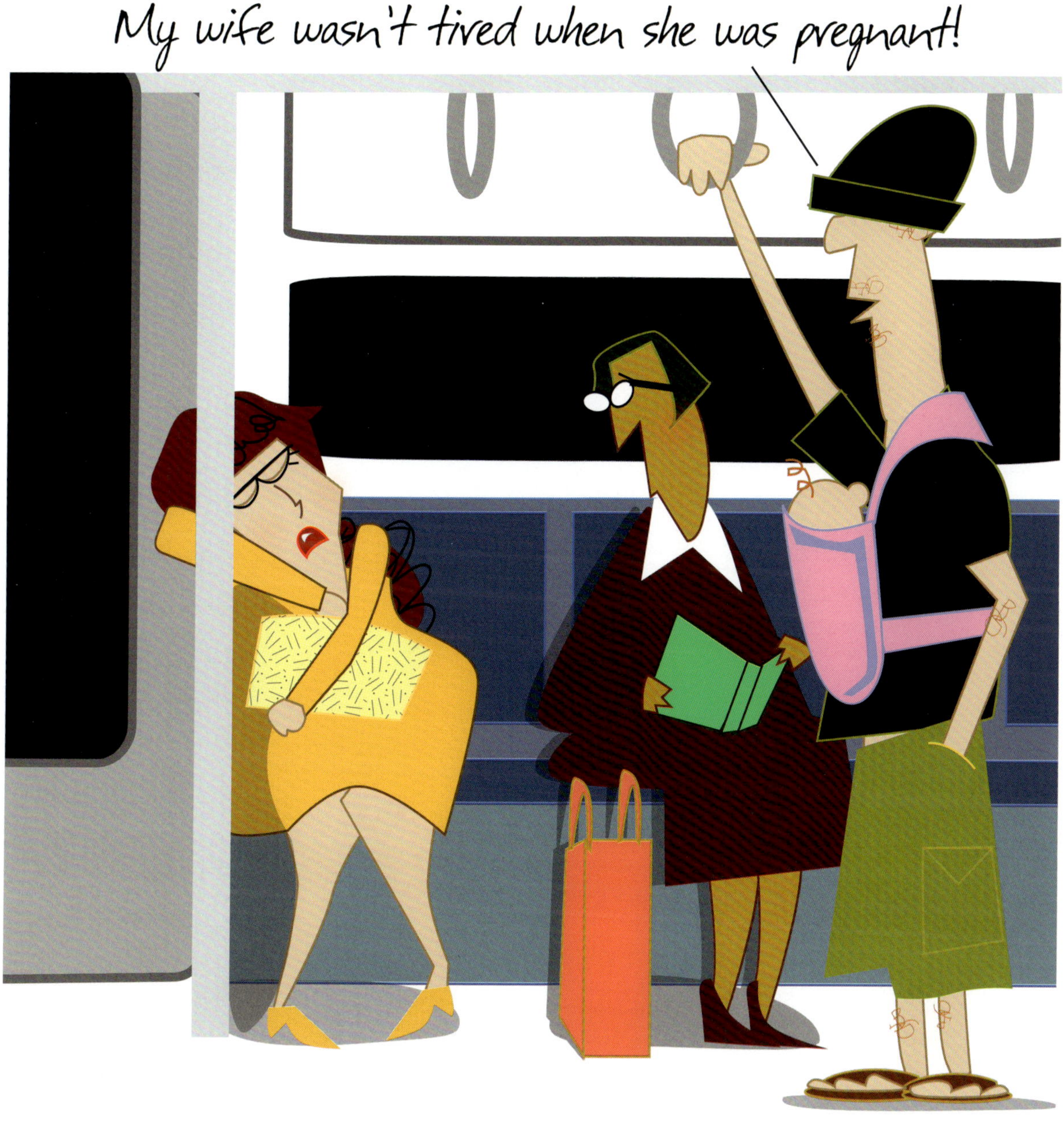
My wife wasn't tired when she was pregnant!

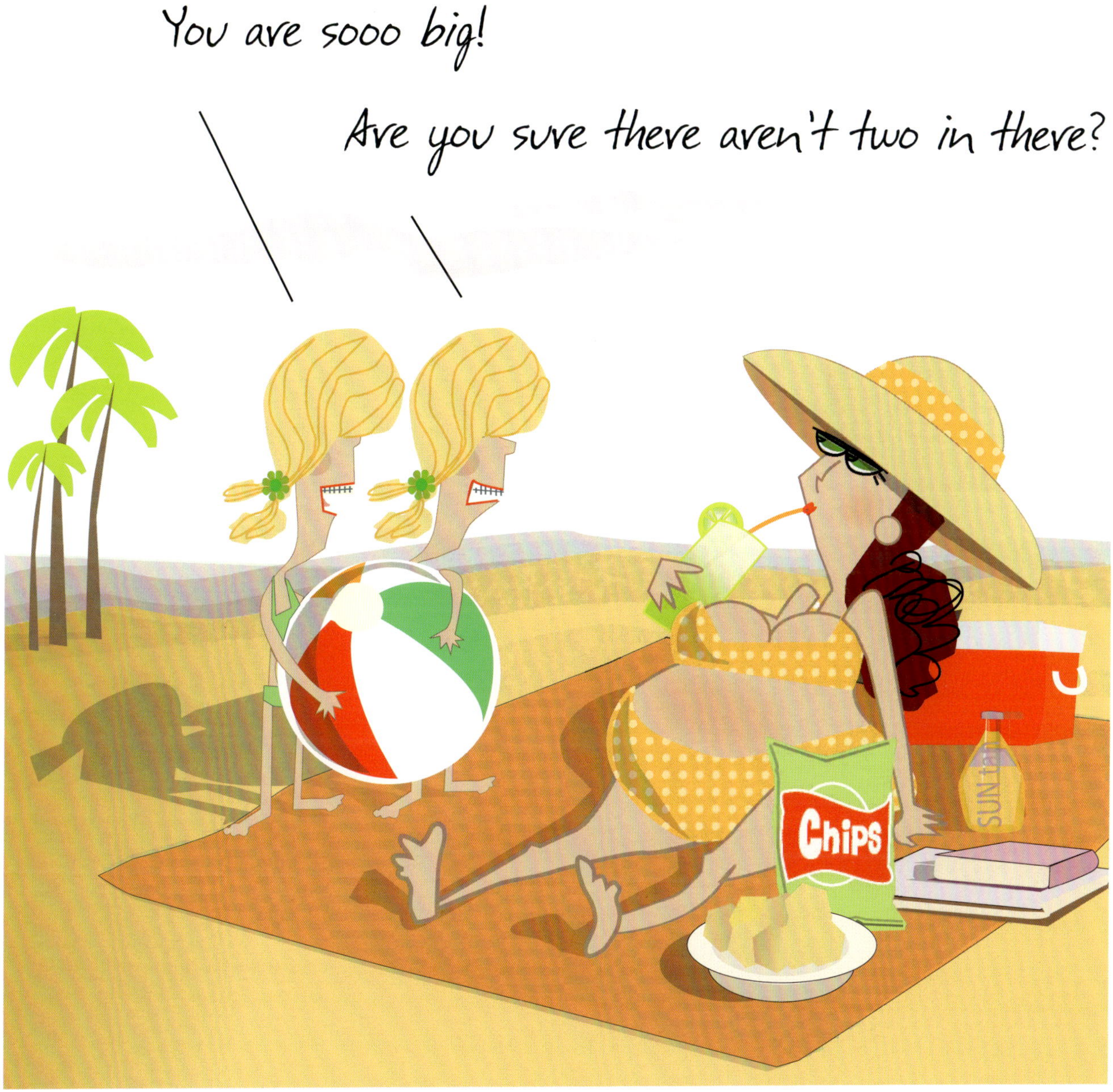
You are sooo big!
Are you sure there aren't two in there?
Chips

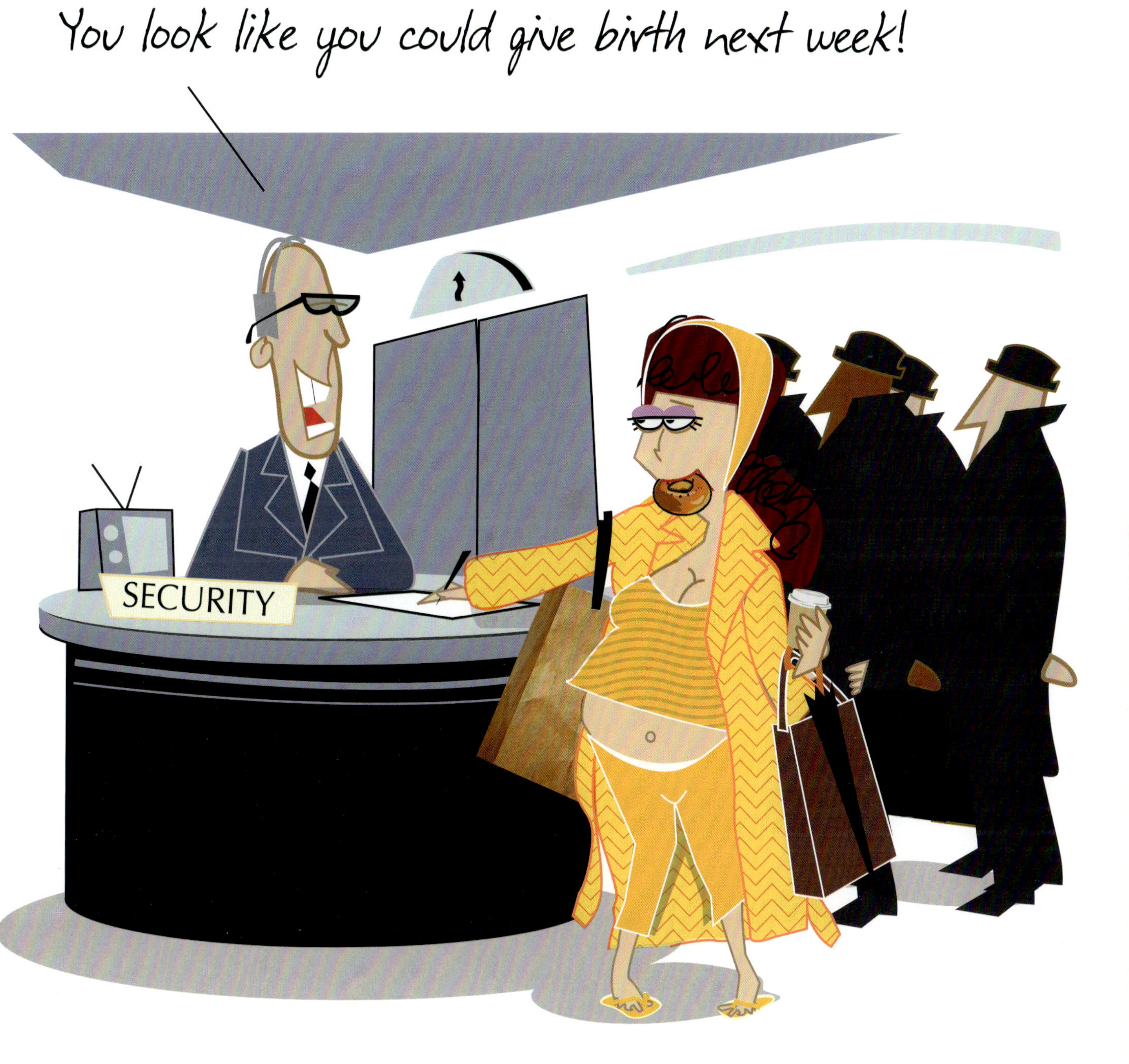
You look like you could give birth next week!
SECURITY

Why can't you fly four weeks before your due date?
Last Trimester

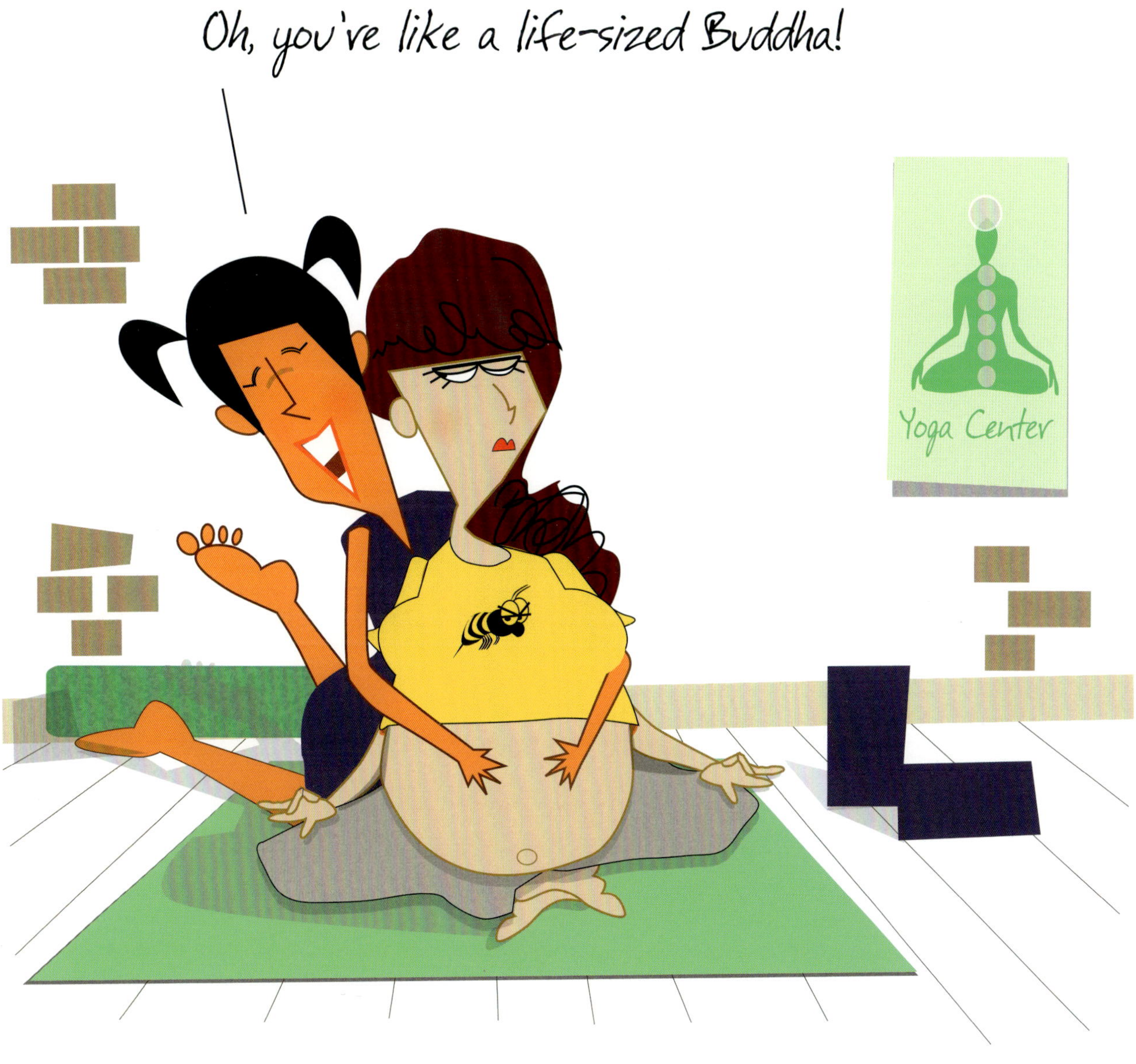
Oh, you've like a life-sized Buddha!
Yoga Center

When your sister was pregnant, she didn't carry as big as you!
Photo Album

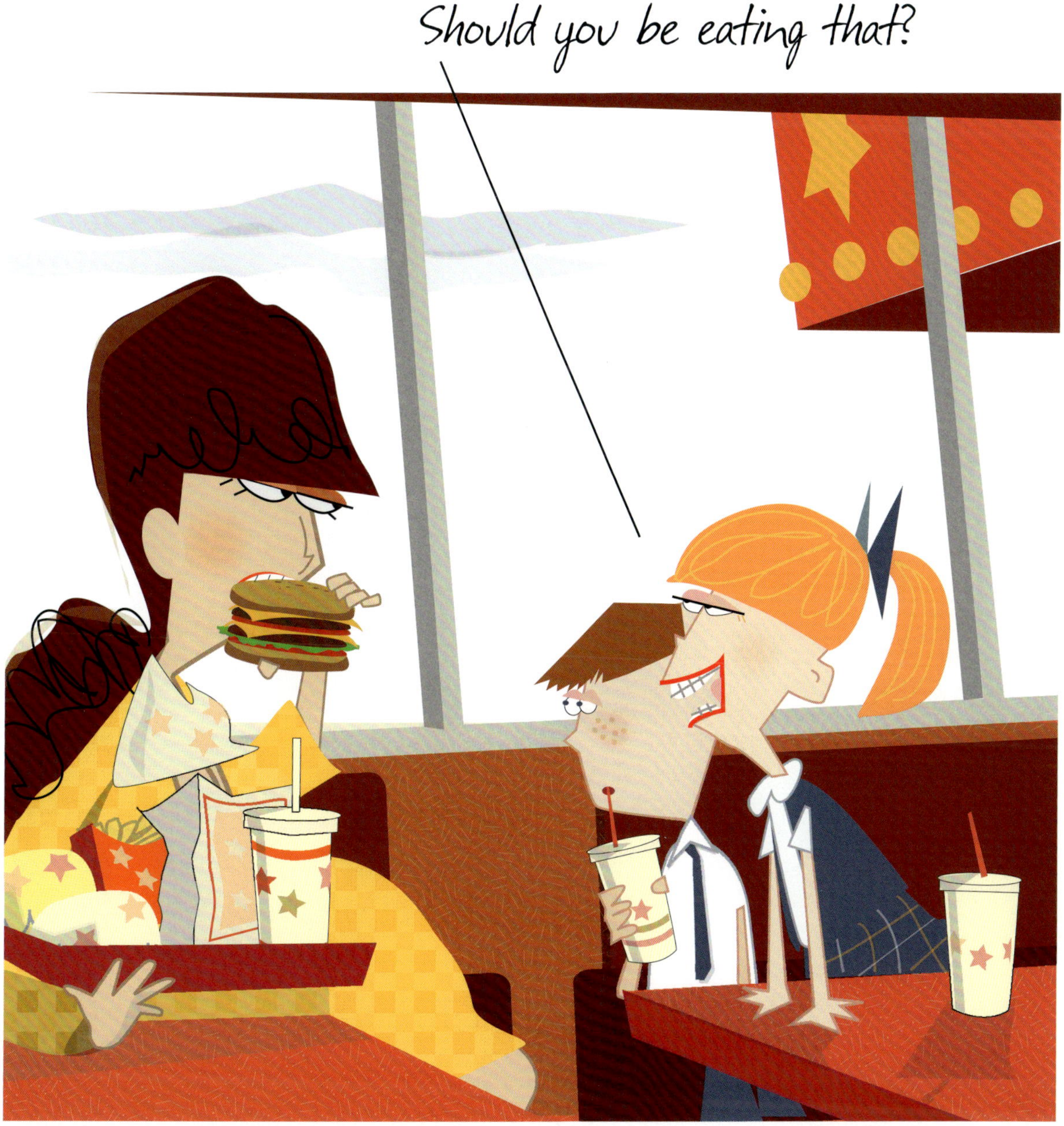
Should you be eating that?

You are carrying everywhere ... your boobs, ass and thighs, so I think it's a girl.

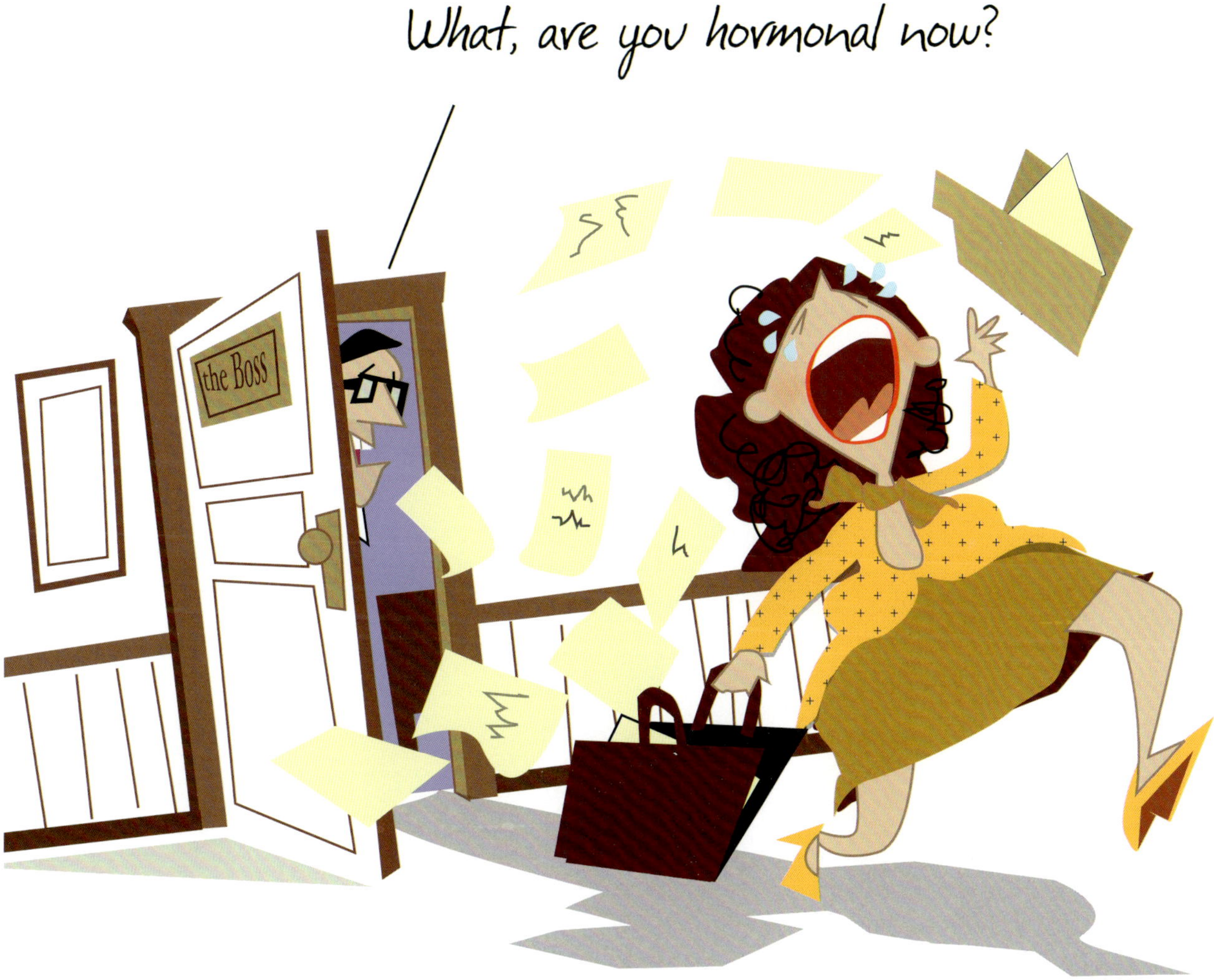
What, are you hormonal now?
the Boss

Your boobs are huge!

LAMAZE CLASS SCHEDULE

Can't you drive to the Chicago appointment?
Chicago
OHIO
PENNA
NEW YORK
ILLINOIS
INDIANA
NEW JERSEY
New York
791.50 Miles
approximately 12 hrs 18 min

You better watch it! You're not the type to exercise.

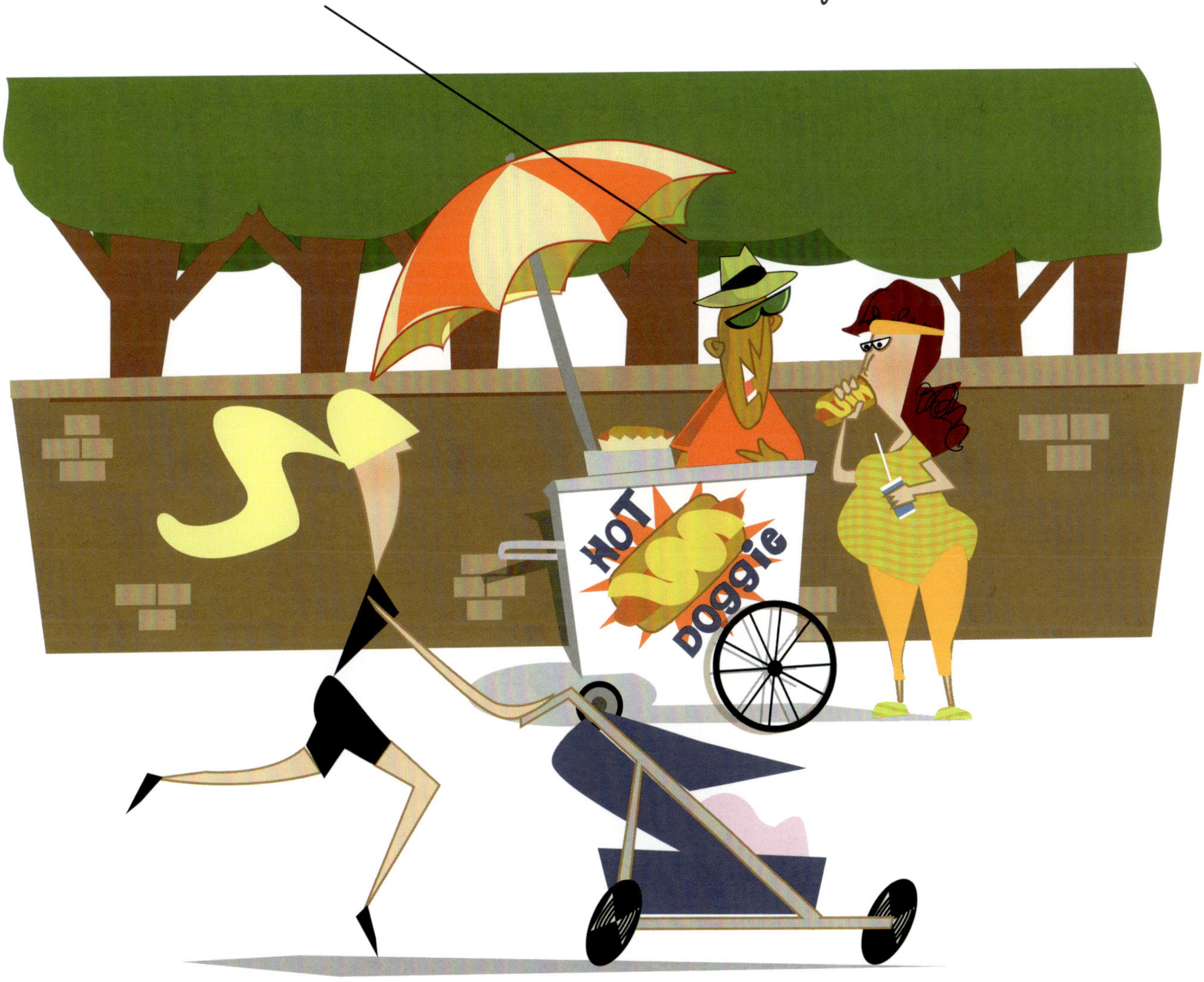

Do you have to take a dump a lot?

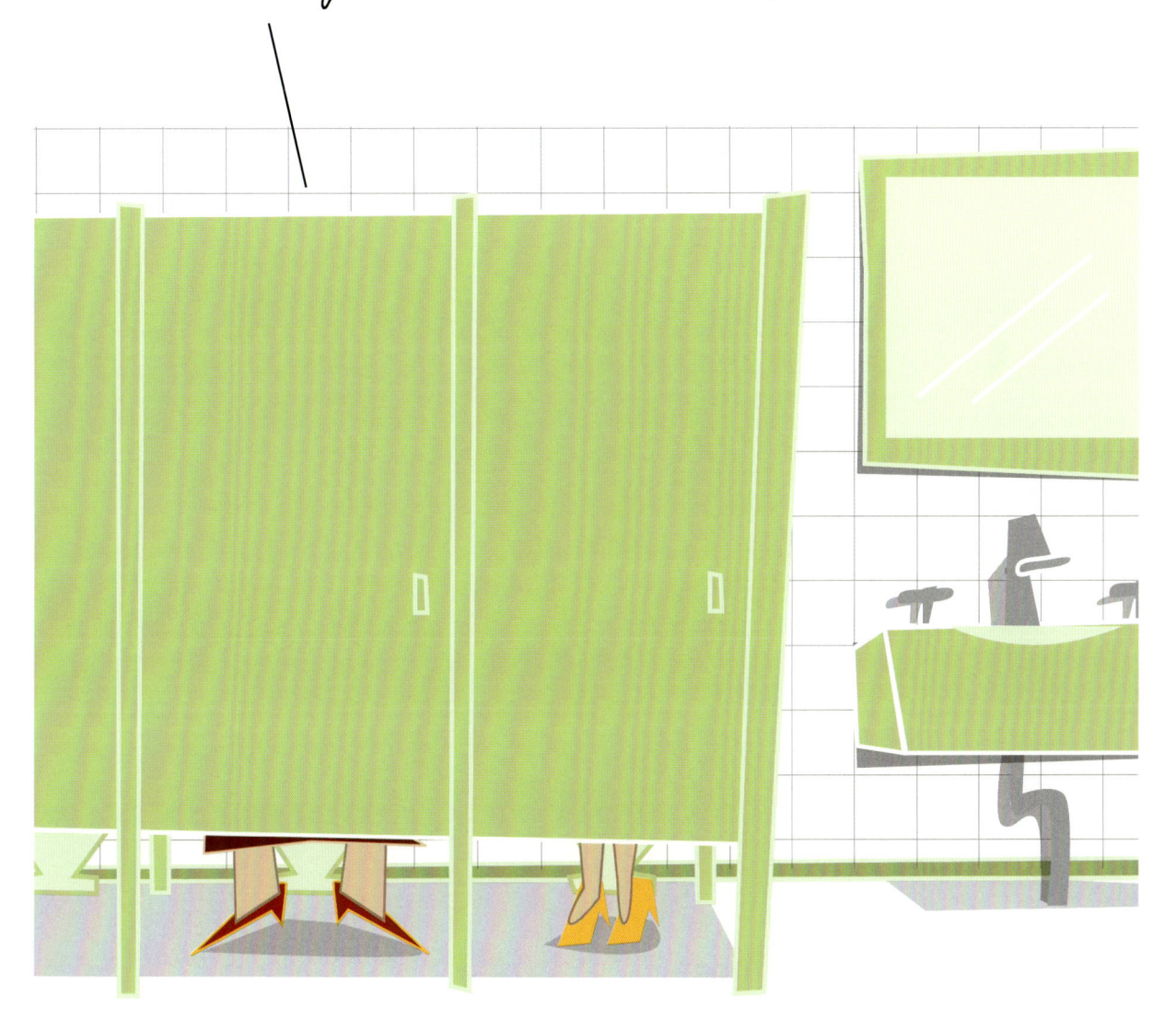

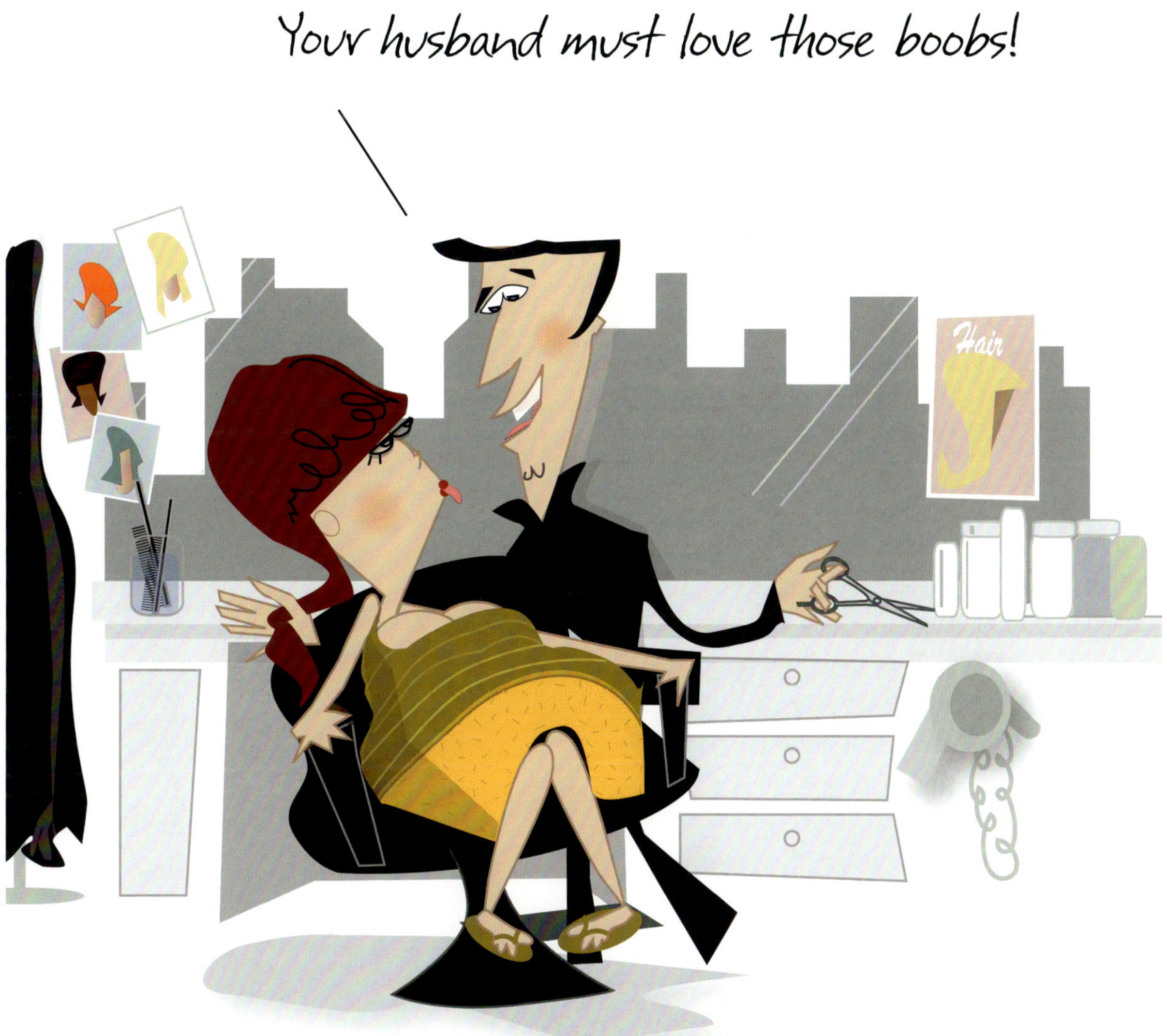
Your husband must love those boobs!
Hair

Your boobs are so huge! It looks like you have enough to feed the whole nursery!

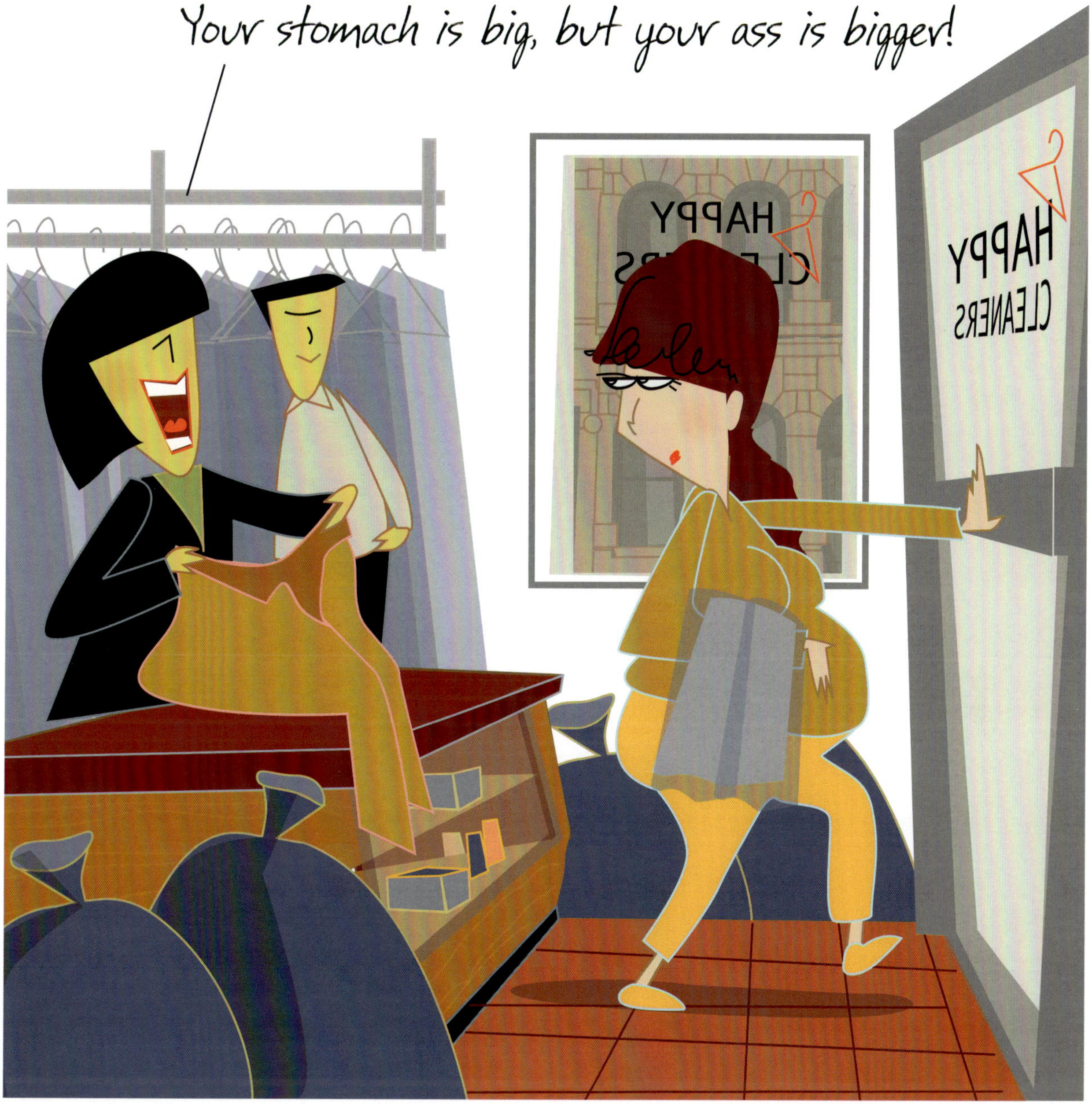
Your stomach is big, but your ass is bigger!
HAPPY CLEANERS

I thought you were pregnant because I noticed your ass getting wider and wider!

I think you're having a girl!
Wait, turn around ...
?
No, you're having a boy!

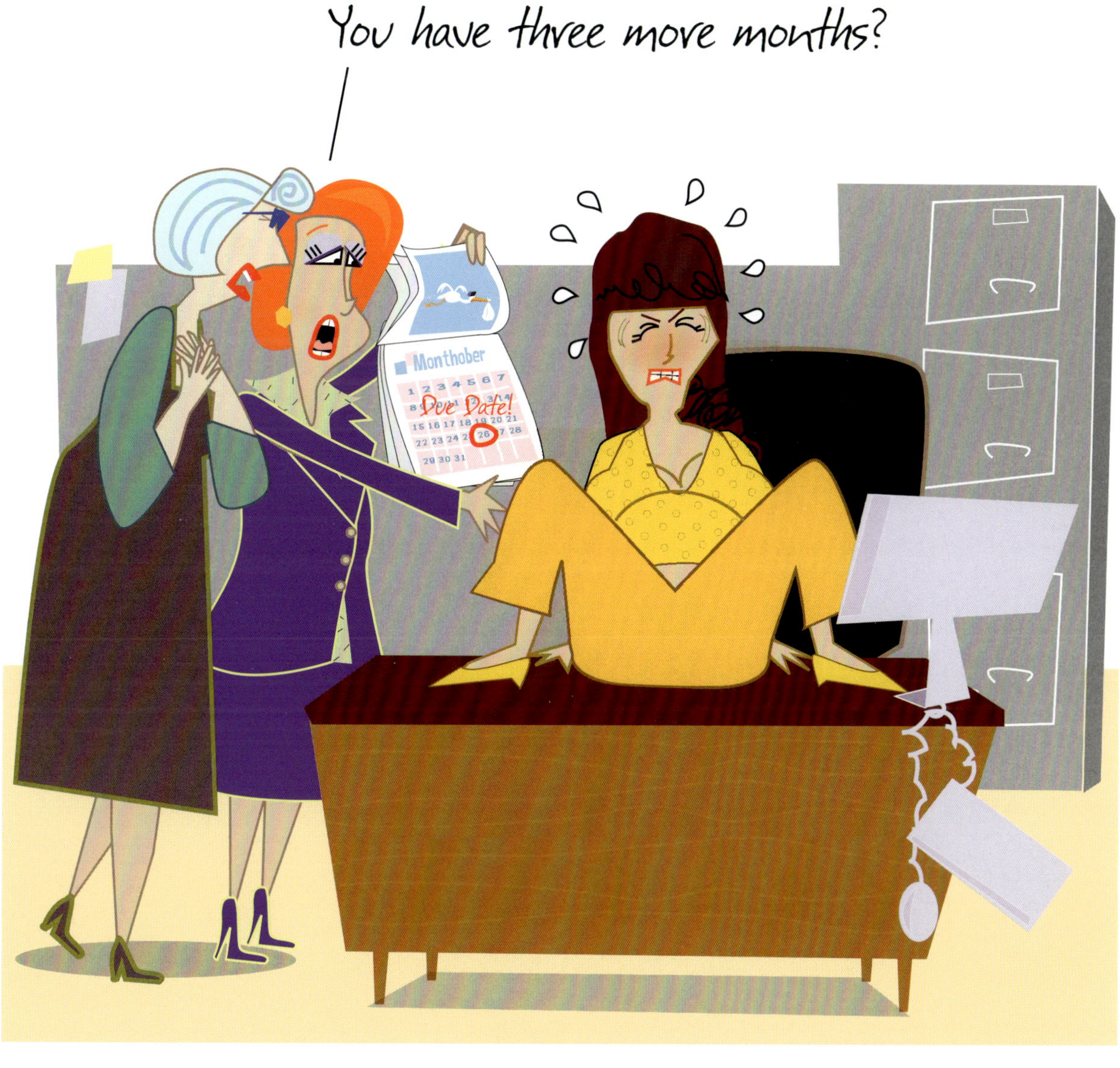
You have three more months?
Monthober
Due Date!

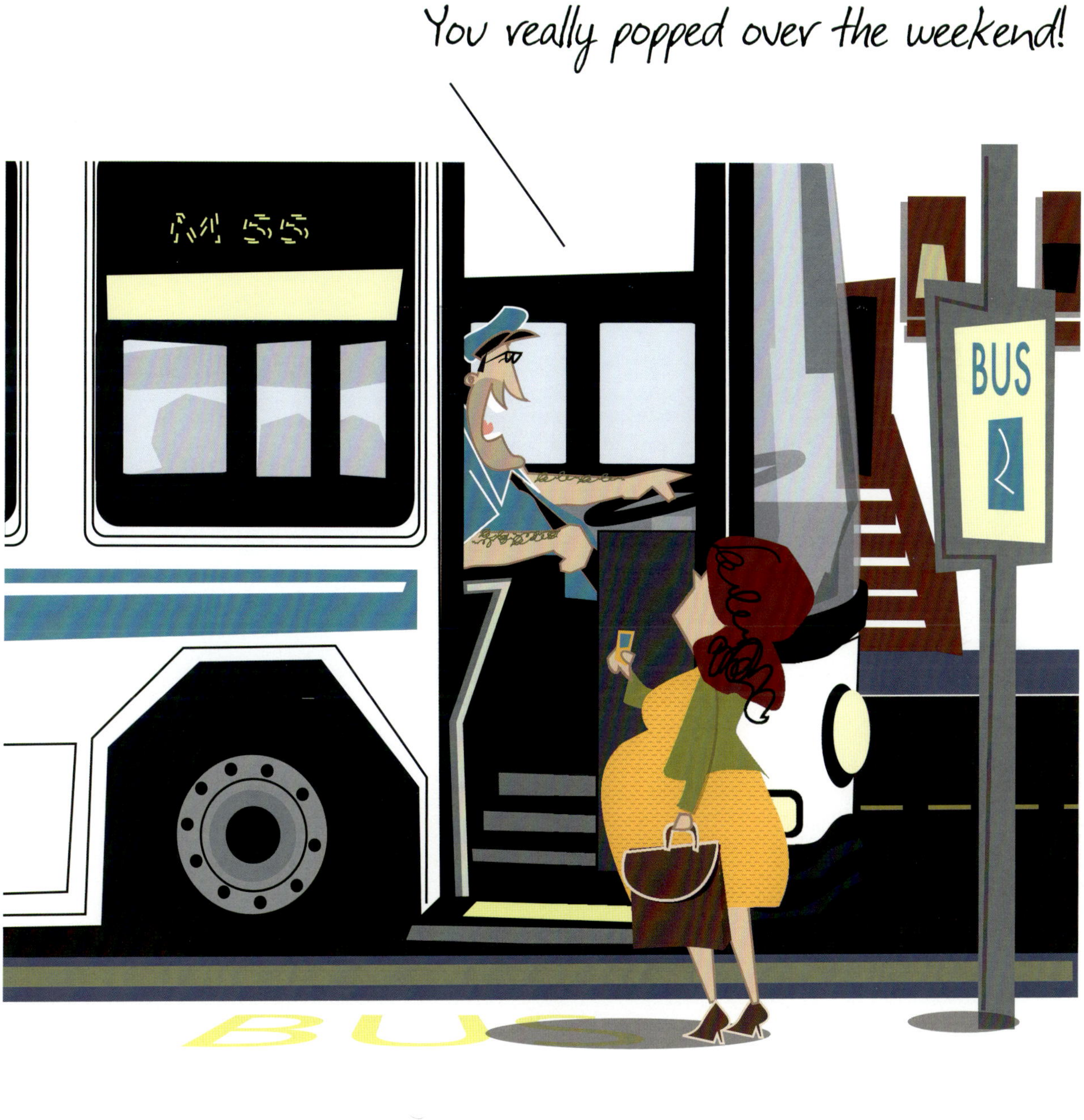
You really popped over the weekend!
BUS

Oh my God! Your boobs are humongous!

Your nose doesn't look that big, so ...
I think you've having a boy!
Is it a Boy or a Girl?

Turn around! Go ahead ... spin around, and I'll tell you if you've having a boy or a girl!
Is it a Boy or a Girl?

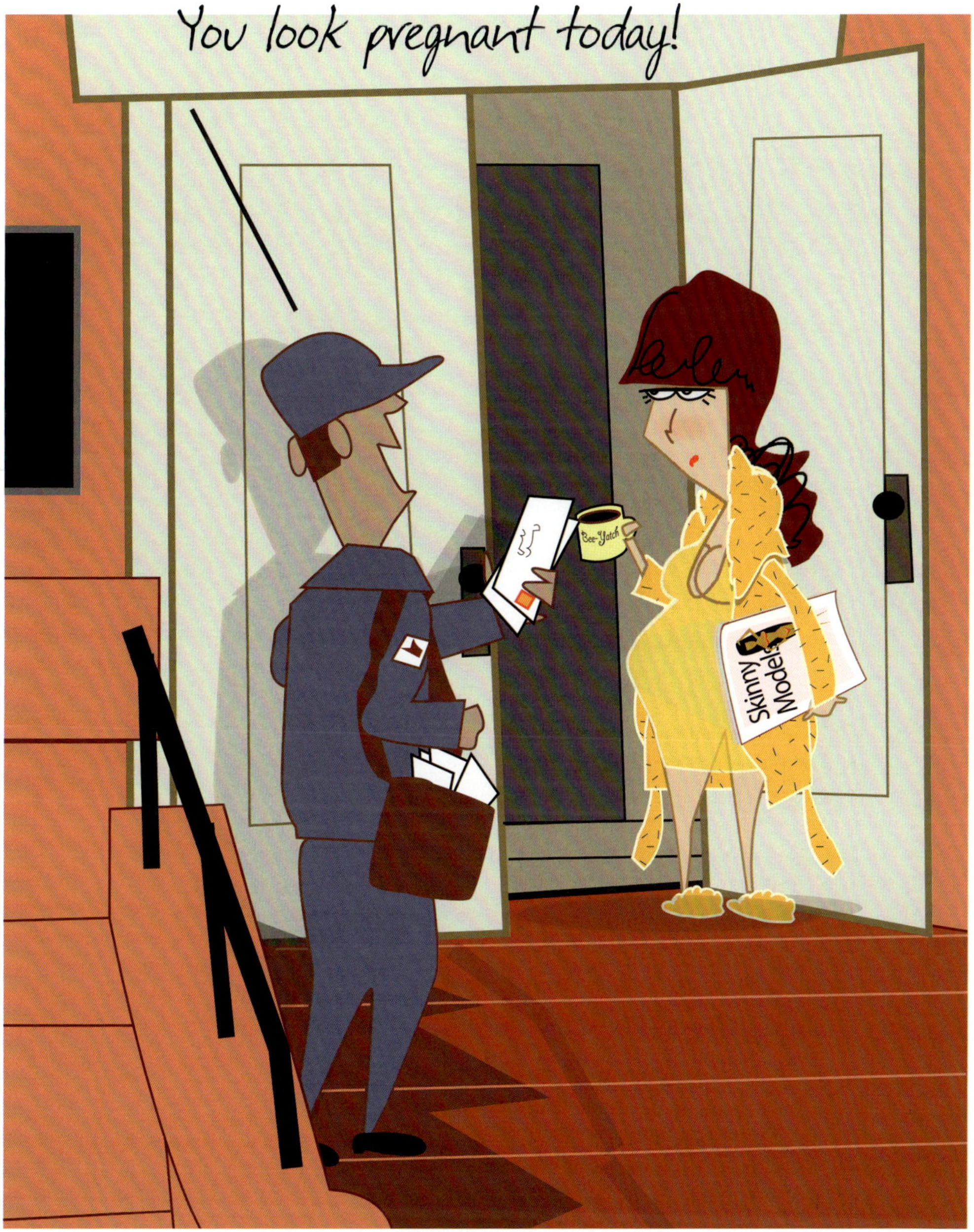
You look pregnant today!
Bee-Yatch
Skinny Models

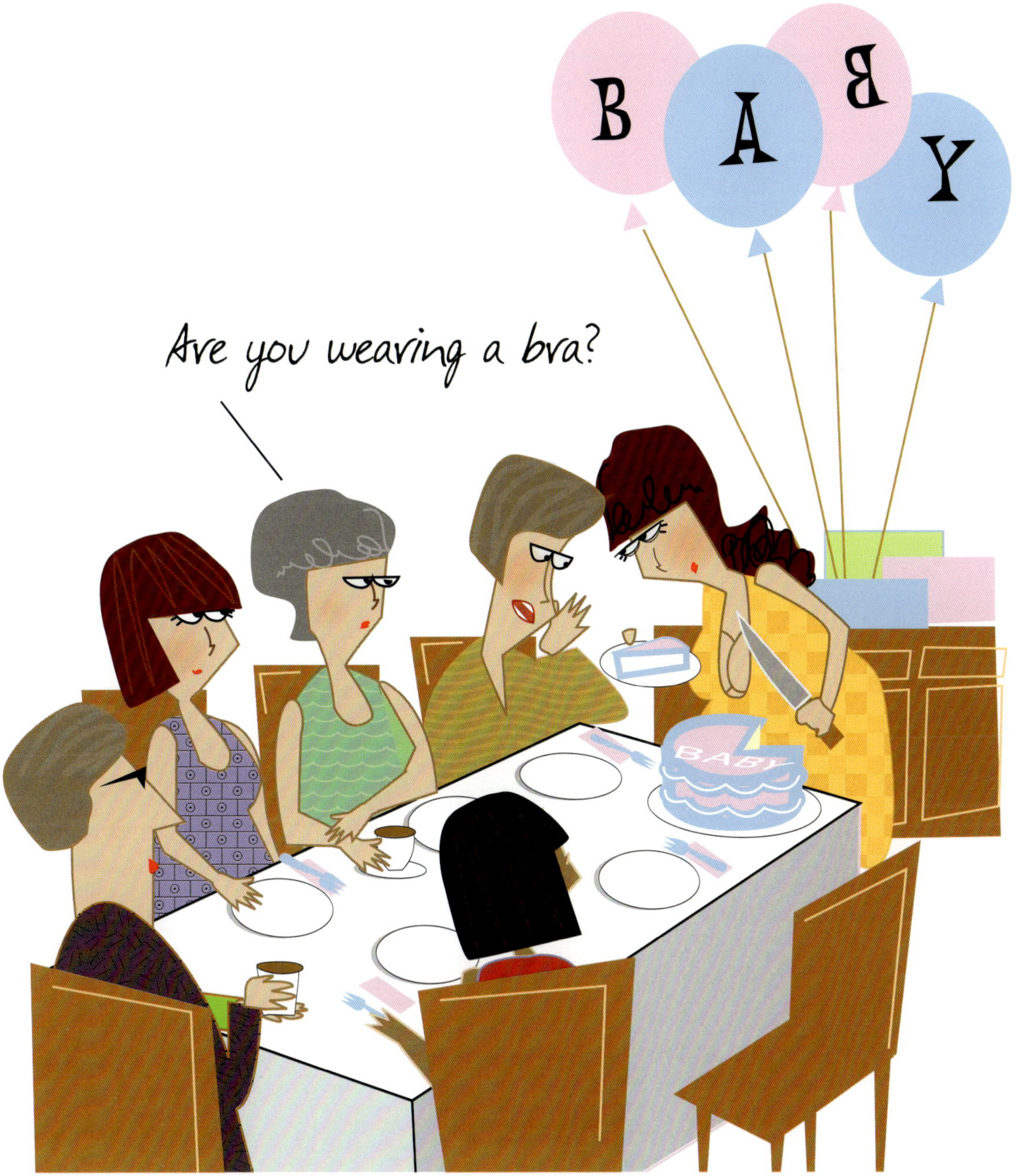

BABY
Are you wearing a bra?
BABY